Walk the Line
With Study Questions

Individual Study
Weekly Small Group

*Plus small-group instruction
and leader's section.*

by
Kris Swiatocho
www.FromHisHands.com Ministries
www.TheSinglesNetwork.org Ministries

Published by:
Yes! Marketing and Design Services, Garner, NC
www.YesMarketingandDesign.com

WALK THE LINE
with Study Questions and Leaders' Section

Copyright ©2014-2018 Kris Swiatocho
Published by Yes! Marketing & Design Services
2664 Timber Drive, Suite 307, Garner, NC 27529
www.YesMarketingandDesign.com

ISBN-13: 978-1987737479

Printed in the United States of America

Dedication

To my Lord and Savior, how grateful I am that you have chosen me to write yet another study to help others in their walk with you.

To Crosswalk.org, an online Christian Magazine who originally published the articles that would eventually be this study, I thank you.

To Leigh Holcomb who did my first set of editing that started the process of conversion into a study, I thank you so much.

To my original study group that included my mom, Stella Davis, our host, Tina Hackett, plus Harold Herman, Laura Masterson, Rozanne Banicki, Tim Ballard, Scott Rice, I am blessed. Thanks for your input each week as we went through the study, allowing the Holy Spirit to speak through you.

To Joseph Northcut with Church Initiative, one of my advisors who offered direction, support, and kindness.

To Lisa Jackson, my editor and friend who encouraged and supported this process.

Psalm 16:5-8
Lord, you alone are my portion and my cup; you make my lot secure. The boundary lines have fallen for me in pleasant places; surely I have a delightful inheritance. I will praise the Lord, who counsels me; even at night my heart instructs me. I keep my eyes always on the Lord. With him at my right hand, I will not be shaken.

Table of Contents

How to do this study as an individual.

Walk the Line Bible study can be used by individuals, small groups, or in a Sunday school structure.

1. Find time to spend with God daily (a time and place where you are least distracted).

2. Begin with prayer; ask for God to reveal His truth to you through His Holy Spirit.

3. Read the chapter and answer the questions. Be prepared to share verbally some of your answers if you are doing the study as a small group.

4. Look up the Scripture references using your own Bible.

5. Write down key points. Ask yourself, "What does this say to me?"

6. Application: What are you going to do now, based on what you have learned? Pray and ask God to identify at least one principle you can take away from this lesson to put into practice.

7. Re-word this principle into a prayer response to God.

Note: If you are reading this book as a small group, take some time to discuss the application to your life, praying for each other through the week. Then, when you meet again, discuss how your week has gone in relation to the principle and prayer applied. If you are a leader, use the leader's section in the back for some additional ideas and Scripture references.

How to do this study as a small group/Sunday school structure.

Prepare

1. Provide the Walk the Line study at the first meeting, or have participants bring their own copy. Walk the Line study can be taught in eight weeks, a chapter each week. However, you could spend the first night getting to know everyone and the last night as a celebration/dinner, expanding it to ten weeks.

2. Decide whether you are going to lead or facilitate. Encourage others to help lead or take turns to develop his/her leadership skills and to provide you with a backup in the event you have to be absent.

3. Decide on the demographics of your group if applicable: all male or female, co-ed, younger or older, etc.

4. Find a good place to have the study if you are using this as a small group. A place that has regulated temperature with the least amount of noise and distraction is best. It should also be a place that is comfortable, safe, has bathrooms, and provides childcare, if needed. Using your church will be favored by most due to its accessibility and resources; however, it might not be the best choice for the lost or spiritually weaker Christians.

5. Plan ahead of time to provide or not provide, childcare. Be sure you have the necessary insurance, facilities, and staff training if childcare is offered. Understand that when you allow children to wander in and out of the study, it causes a distraction; be sensitive to others who don't have children.

6. Before beginning the study, plan the dates, length of each session, time, and where your small group will meet. Be respectful of your participants' personal schedules by starting and ending on time. Make sure you communicate this with your group and why it's important. If people have questions that could lead you in other directions, or seem to monopolize the time, tell them you can answer their questions more thoroughly after the study has ended.

7. Other distractions; Before beginning the study, ask people to use the restroom, turn off cell phones, get food/drink, etc.

8. Market the Walk the Line study ahead of time. Promote your study group to your church and throughout the community. E-mail public service announcements to local radio and TV stations. Put flyers and posters up on the walls at restaurants and grocery stores. Promote on Facebook and other social media. Be sure to have a way for them to contact you for an RSVP by a certain date. Go to www.FromHisHands.org or www.TheSinglesNetwork.org for free marketing materials you can download.

During
1. Decide on the guidelines for the group. For example: tardiness, absenteeism, bringing children, not doing the necessary reading/assignment, sharing what is discussed outside the group, etc.

2. Understand that if you use this study for Sunday school, you might have some limitations during your discussions. Keep the group to a maximum of 10 people, or break it down into smaller groups of three or four during discussion times.

3. If you don't know your attendees, have them fill out a survey that might include how they found out about the study, their church name, marital status, hobbies, e-mail, etc. This provides a way to contact them during the study and, afterwards, for future events. Contact your group each week to check on them, encourage them, and tell them you look forward to seeing them again.

4. Have them sit in a circle or at a table to enhance communication. Start with an icebreaker, a warm-up exercise, or another way of getting to know each person. You can purchase a huge list of icebreakers at www.FromHisHands.com or www.TheSinglesNetwork.org.

5. Remind people of the purpose of this study (what God has given you as the vision).

6. Keep things upbeat and positive even in the midst of more serious topics of discussion.

7. Open with prayer. (As time goes on, you can ask others to open and/or close in prayer.) Start on time and end on time.

8. Encourage people to bring their Bibles and take notes each week. Encourage them to use a Bible dictionary or concordance if needed. Understand that each person will be at a different place in his/her spiritual walk.

9. Provide refreshments, extra paper, Bibles, pens, books, etc.

10. As a leader, you should prepare your lesson early, allowing time for the Holy Spirit to guide you in teaching the study. Be creative; use objects, jokes, music, videos...whatever might add value to the lesson. For additional help, see the last section of this study.

11. Encourage everyone to share their answers and/or questions. Call on individuals who do not normally share. Try to involve all the attendees. In private ask those who talk the most to allow others the chance to participate.

Note: Some people believe you should tell participants they do not have to talk or pray if they don't feel comfortable. I believe, however, that it should be a goal to help them through this. As they feel comfortable and accepted, I believe they will feel like sharing.

12. Teach others/disciple: Remember, we are all commanded by Jesus to go and make disciples. Empower people with options to help teach or facilitate, lead small-group discussions, prayer, mid-week follow-up, etc.

Close/Follow-up

1. Close by briefly discussing the week ahead. Make assignments or tell of your expectations for the week. When they return the following week, be sure to go over their assignment and/or share about their week. Note: For larger groups, you can break into small groups for this discussion.

2. Do a large-group prayer or break people into prayer partners for the next several weeks of the study and have the groups pray after each lesson. Encourage them to get each other's phone numbers, so they can call and pray for one another during the week. Note: Pair up men with men and women with women.

3. At the end of the small-group study, consider having a special dinner or party to celebrate. Use some of what people have learned as a part of the final celebration.

4. Ask the group leader whether they would like to continue into another study or take a break. Do a follow-up survey on the study and/or your teaching style.

Why Walk the Line Study?

So many times in life I would find myself saying the phrase, "There's a fine line between this word and that word." Often it was when I was discipling someone or in general conversation. I found that people would use some of the same words to mean the same thing when in all actuality they were different. That there was a fine line between the two. And that fine line was often where one word was "self-focused" and the other was "other-focused". One word was about your own agenda, needs, and wants, and the other was about lifting, encouraging, or supporting the other person. So if you could determine the difference, then perhaps you would use the right word at the right time. And then the fine line wouldn't be so fine.

So after years of hearing myself say this phrase, God told me I should start writing about them. At the time, I was a featured writer with Crosswalk.com and so I offered the series to them and they accepted. From the series, I then converted the articles to a Bible study calling it "Walk the Line." I then brought together a focus group of singles and marrieds who did the study with me, allowing input, edits, etc. So, I pray you enjoy the study, learning the differences with common words we use every day, in the hopes you grow closer to God and his direction for your life.

—Kris Swiatocho

Chapter 1:
Walk the Line: Judging versus Accountability

Can You Believe What He Said?

Overheard one Sunday at church: "Oh, look over there. She is dressed like a tramp again. Can someone please tell her that we do not want to see her bellybutton anymore? Did you see that Mr. Jones with some new woman and her kids? I think he must have a different woman each week. I don't think that is right with God. Where have all the bulletins gone? That church secretary is no good. We need to fire her. What did you say, Pastor? We need to pray for the Smith family again? Shoot, all we do is pray for their finances. Maybe they should get off their duffs and get a job and stop asking the church for help all the time."

Does any of this sound familiar? I know I have thought and said similar things a few times in my life. In the South, where I live, we have a way of getting into people's business and calling it concern. We say we are praying for the person with other believers but in reality, we are just spreading gossip. We want to hold them accountable in truth but end up judging them in lies. Don't get me wrong, there are some folks that are concerned and do care. I have found that a "fine line" exists between judging people and holding them accountable. I think most people get the two ideas confused. Many people say they are holding someone accountable when in fact they are making a judgment. How do you know the difference?

Accountability is:

Judgment is:

Q: When have you ever felt judged? Share.

The Fine Line Revealed:
Let's first establish what accountability is: Accountability is something God established to help us grow in Him. If holding us accountable has been done correctly by others, the results should be evident by:

• our attitude,
• our walk with God,
• our faithfulness, and
• the increasing awareness of our sin.

We will become:

• more humble,
• more teachable, and
• more willing to change to be like Christ.

Read Matthew 12:35-36
The good man brings good things out of the good stored up in him, and the evil man brings evil things out of the evil stored up in him. But I tell you that men will have to give account on the day of judgment for every careless word they have spoken.

We are all accountable to God. As we spend time in the Word, serve, tithe, pray, have a great attitude, etc. we are storing up good things. Out of a good walk comes a good witness.

Q: What does a good witness mean to you?

Read Hebrews 13:17
Obey your leaders and submit to their authority. They keep watch over you as men who must give an account. Obey them so that their work will be a joy, not a burden, for that would be of no advantage to you.

We are accountable to those we serve or under whom we work. God has placed them over us to teach and guide us, even if this means some of them are not Christians. We are still accountable to those in authority (our bosses, government, police, parents, etc.). In turn, they are being held accountable by God for how they hold us accountable.

Q: To whom are you accountable in your work, ministry, club, etc.? How difficult has it been to be held accountable?

Read Romans 15:14
I myself am convinced, my brothers, that you yourselves are full of goodness, complete in knowledge and competent to instruct one another.

As Christians, we are also accountable to each other. It's one thing to be held accountable by God and by those in authority over us, but to be accountable to another believer? Boy, that can be hard. So many of us won't hold each other accountable because we don't want to come across as judgmental. We don't want to come across like we don't have our own junk. God commands us to hold others accountable, but He has given us instructions (see below) on how to do it so that it isn't judgment.

Q: When have you been held accountable by a brother or sister in Christ and you didn't like it?

Q: Sometimes we fear holding others accountable due to knowing how the person might react. Share a time when you held someone accountable, what happened?

Steps on how to hold someone accountable in the Lord:

Read Psalm 139:23-24
Search me, O God, and know my heart; test me and know my anxious thoughts. See if there is any offensive way in me, and lead me in the way everlasting.

1. Look at yourself first and make sure your heart is in the right place before you hold anyone else accountable for sin. It's not that you won't have your own sin, but are you aware of it? Are you working on it?

Holding others accountable usually happens at a point when they aren't even aware they are sinning or how their sin is affecting others. Accountability brings awareness. If people know you are humble, they are more likely to receive your guidance.

Q: What is God asking you to change about yourself first?

Read James 1:19-20
My dear brothers, take note of this: Everyone should be quick to listen, slow to speak and slow to become angry, for man's anger does not bring about the righteous life that God desires.

2. Before you can hold anyone accountable, you must have a relationship with that person based on trust. That is why our accountability can sometimes come across as gossip or judgment. When there is no relationship, no trust, people have a hard time taking direction from others. If we don't have a relationship, we have no idea what might be going on in someone's life, so we make assumptions. These assump-

tions start in our minds and quickly become verbal. Once airborne, they can spread like a virus causing major damage. We must be willing to listen and understand as much as we can about a person's life.

Q: What type of relationship should you have with someone to hold them accountable?

Q: If we don't have a relationship, what can quickly happen?

Maybe the lady in church dresses so provocatively because she has had a horrible upbringing. Maybe she has never had anyone come beside her and be her friend. Maybe the man who came to church each week with a different family is really ministering to them. Maybe they are his neighbors, his family, or people from a local shelter. But how would you rightly interpret the situation without knowing that person?

Grace alert: Don't ever forget where you were when God found you, where He saved you, where He poured into you (and still does). The Scriptures provide guidance on how to walk the "fine line" of relationships with others. You might also approach the person with sharing your own struggles and how God has been/is working on you, too, and that your desire to bring up this sin is to help them grow in the Lord.

Read 1 John 4:21
And He has given us this command: Whoever loves God must also love his brother.

3. Hold others accountable in love. You want to know where the fine line is between judgment and accountability? It's in love. When you see the sin of someone you love, it should break your heart. It should make you sad because you hurt for them. You see where their sin is taking them because you have been there. You want to help them, not hurt them. You want them to break free from the sin. You want them to experience freedom and victory in Christ. Judging someone is more about being self-focused. It's easier to judge someone else than deal with our own mess. It's more about our heart—holding someone accountable requires us to deal with our own junk first. Holding someone accountable is being other-focused.

Q: Who is the object of focus in judgment?

Q: Who is the object of focus in accountability?

Read Galatians 5:25-6:2
Since we live by the Spirit, let us keep in step with the Spirit. Let us not become conceited, provoking and envying each other. Brothers, if someone is caught in a sin, you who are spiritual should restore him gently. But watch yourself, or you also may be tempted. Carry each other's burdens, and in this way you will fulfill the law of Christ.

Read Romans 15:1-2
We who are strong ought to bear with the failings of the weak and not to please ourselves. Each of us should please his neighbor for his good, to build him up.

4. Hold others accountable in keeping with God's Spirit. We must approach the person gently, praying the entire time that God will have them receive what we say. First, encourage and give praise on what they are doing for the Lord and how they are making a difference. Let them know how much we care about them. After sharing with them our thoughts, encourage them to hold us accountable as well. This will encourage an open relationship of trust.

Large group exercise: Break into 2 groups and practice holding each other accountable.

Scenario: 1
Let's pretend person "A" is spending money you know she doesn't have. She has shared her struggle on more than one occasion to the class about how she isn't able to pay her bills. You have even helped her a time or two

through a class donation—person A doesn't know you personally. One Sunday, a group of you went shopping and you noticed person "A" bought an expensive pair of earrings. How would you handle this? How would you hold her accountable?

Scenario: 2

Let's pretend person "A" is spending money you know she doesn't have. She has shared her struggle on more than one occasion to you personally about how she isn't able to pay her bills. You have even helped her a time or two. One Sunday, a group of you went shopping and you noticed person "A" bought an expensive pair of earphones. How would you handle this? How would you hold her accountable?

Read Matthew 7:1-2
Do not judge, or you too will be judged. For in the same way you judge others, you will be judged, and with the measure you use, it will be measured to you.

5. Judgment is reserved for God. Only God knows man's heart to the core. Only God knows what a man has said to Him and whether repentance for a sin is true. We have to be careful that our comments, our thoughts, and our actions do not appear to be judging someone. Our advice will always come across as judgment until we take the time to get to know someone, to build a relationship with him or her, to build up trust. After the relationship has formed, he/she will be more likely to accept our advice.

WHAT ARE YOU GOING TO WALK AWAY WITH?
What is God saying to you right now?

[Close in prayer; option to list prayer requests here so you can pray through the week for each other.]

ASSIGNMENT:
1. Pray and ask God to reveal what sin in your life needs to be removed.

2. Pray and ask God to show you anyone that needs accountability for their sin.

3. Pray about the situation first. If someone's sin or negative action is affecting your ministry, your church, your community, your family, etc., you will have to deal with it at some point. If you are not sure about the situation, you can involve your pastor or other trusted counselor—but be careful with whom you discuss it, as not every battle in life is yours to fight.

Note: Sometimes I don't feel led to be the one to approach that person. Instead I leave it for God to deal with. God may have someone else in mind that might be better equipped but I can continue to pray for that person. Also remember not to share it with others as it can quickly become gossip.

Remember, accountability in life is not only about becoming a better person, a stronger Christian and follower of Jesus, it's also about building up the body of Christ so that we are all stronger against the enemy. When someone comes along your way (in love and sometimes not in love) and holds you accountable, then listen, pray and discern if it's something you need to deal with or change, and ask for forgiveness.

Read 1 Corinthians 16:13-16
Be on your guard; stand firm in the faith; be men of courage; be strong. Do everything in love. You know that the household of Stephanas were the first converts in Achaia, and they have devoted themselves to the service of the saints. I urge you, brothers, to submit to such as these and to everyone who joins in the work, and labors at it.

WALK THE LINE

Chapter 2:
Walk the Line: Happiness versus Joy

I Know Marriage Would Make Me Happy

"Lord, please bring me a spouse. I know marriage can be hard but I truly believe being married will bring me joy. I would be so happy and complete. I am just so unhappy being single."

"Lord, I have worked so hard at my job and I need that promotion. I need more money. I need to buy things, go interesting places, and dress better. I know I would be much happier with a bigger bank account."

"Lord, please, I pray with all my heart that my house loan gets approved. A house would provide a place to have a Bible study and invite family. I know having a home will make me happy and bring joy to so many."

"Lord, I don't like this storm. Bills are up to my eyeballs, my health isn't great, my family is too demanding, and I am struggling. I am not happy. Please take these troubles away so I can be happy again, so that I will have joy."

Does any of this sound familiar? How many times have we lived our lives based on circumstances? How many times have those circumstances dictated our relationship with God, with others? I have had my own issues over the years with understanding the "fine line" between happiness and joy. I have prayed for a spouse, prayed for my finances, and prayed that God would take away my pain. Why? So that life would be better. So that life would be happier. I mean, who wants to go around in pain and misery all the time? But what God has been able to show me has had far greater value. He has taught and continues to teach me that happiness is not all that it's cracked up to be. Happiness is based on our circumstances. Circumstances that can change like the wind.

True joy is based on our relationship with God. God has shown me through my earnest seeking of happiness, that I should pursue the greater thing—His joy! This way I could be happy in all situations. I could be happy without a spouse, without the bigger home or new car, without more stuff, and without that juicy cheeseburger and fries. So, what does "happiness versus joy" mean to you? Is there really that much of a difference? Where is that "fine line"?

Happiness is:

Joy is:

Read 1 Kings 4:20
The people of Judah and Israel were as numerous as the sand
on the seashore; they ate, they drank and they were happy.

Q: What does this scripture mean to you?

The Fine Line Revealed:

HAPPINESS
Happiness is based on circumstances. Don't get me wrong,
there is nothing wrong with being happy. I love being happy.
I love getting excited about getting new stuff or a friend coming for a visit or a cute guy flirting with me. I love getting a
massage, eating at my favorite restaurant or making jewelry.
Happiness is not a sin. But knowing that the emotion won't
last is the issue. Circumstances change and as a result, happiness will as well.

**Q: How often have you said or heard, "I just want to be
happy"? Why do we say this? What are we really wanting?**

Read Matthew 6:19-20

"Do not store up for yourselves treasures on earth, where moth and rust destroy, and where thieves break in and steal. But store up for yourselves treasures in heaven, where moth and rust do not destroy, and where thieves do not break in and steal."

Q: Share a time when you valued something and it was stolen, taken away, got broken, etc. What were the circumstances and how did you feel?

Happiness is temporary. Stuff gets old, rusts, or falls apart. Friends and family leave. Food gets eaten. You have to wait until you can afford another massage. Being happy is like standing on a mountaintop. My mother once told me the mountaintop is a tiny place. The journey up the mountain and then down the mountain is where the real growth takes place. As we walk up the mountain, our muscles are tested. We have to sometimes rest, pray, ask for help to continue the journey. Coming down, the path is easier but still has some danger. This is a time to evaluate the journey, look around and assess what worked and what didn't work. Then comes the valley, the lowest point where life seems the hardest. This is where we sometimes think God isn't listening, but it really comes down to perspective—the valley is where the grass grows the greenest and things only grow greener if there's plenty of fertilizer!

Q: When have you had to climb the mountain? Share.

Q: When have you had to come down the mountain?
Share.

Q: What was your experience on the mountaintop?
Share.

Q: What has the valley—the area between the mountains—been like? Share.

Read 1 Peter 5:8-9
"Be self-controlled and alert. Your enemy the devil prowls around like a roaring lion looking for someone to devour. Resist him, standing firm in the faith, because you know that your brothers throughout the world are undergoing the same kind of sufferings."

Happiness will not fill you or take away your trouble. We are constantly looking for the world to fill us. We want more stuff, more money, more dates, more, more, more. Happiness becomes like an addictive drug and we have this enormous craving for it.

Q: Do you remember when the enemy tempted Jesus?

Read Matthew 4:1-11
Then Jesus was led by the Spirit into the wilderness to be tempted by the devil. After fasting forty days and forty nights, he was hungry. The tempter came to him and said, "If you are the Son of God, tell these stones to become bread." Jesus answered, "It is written: 'Man shall not live on bread alone, but on every word that comes from the mouth of God.'" Then the devil took him to the holy city and had him stand on the highest point of the temple. "If you are the Son of God," he said, "throw yourself down. For it is written: '"He will command his angels concerning you, and they will lift you up in their hands, so that you will not strike your foot against a stone."'" Jesus answered him, "It is also written: 'Do not put the Lord your God

to the test.'" Again, the devil took him to a very high mountain and showed him all the kingdoms of the world and their splendor. "All this I will give you," he said, "if you will bow down and worship me." Jesus said to him, "Away from me, Satan! For it is written: 'Worship the Lord your God, and serve him only.'" Then the devil left him, and angels came and attended him.

Q: With what did the devil tempt Jesus?

Power, stuff, food, and wealth—the enemy knows our flesh is weak and prowls about, waiting for the next time to jump on us and stir those cravings! Knowing this should help us in making decisions about what brings us true joy. Being happy about seeing a friend, getting a date, buying a new outfit is fine as long as we know it is not why we are living on this earth. Being happy will not take away the trouble. It may only mask it for a while. True joy, which comes from God, can happen in the midst of our troubles.

Q: What does the scripture say we must do in regards to our joy, meaning to keep our faith and be steadfast in Christ?

Q: How has the devil affected your joy at times?

Read Ecclesiastes 7:14
When times are good, be happy; but when times are bad, consider: God has made the one as well as the other. Therefore, a man cannot discover anything about his future.

Q: Knowing this truth, how does that help in your perspective on life?

JOY

Happiness is self-focused versus God-focused. Every day most of us are seeking to just be happy. We want a great day at work with no issues. We want our kids to do well in school and be well-liked. We want to get along with family members. We want our washing machines to work, quick accessibility to the remote, great weather, easy traffic, and no lines at the grocery store. But what does God want? Maybe He has allowed that pain in your marriage to draw you both to Him. Maybe the lines are long because God wants you to start a conversation with the person beside you about

Christ. Maybe the weather will cause you to drive slower and stop texting. Maybe not finding the remote will cause you to spend some quality time with your family, or with God. We should be God-seekers versus happiness-seekers. What is great about seeking God is realizing that His desire for us is to experience His joy! Joy that will transcend even those temporary circumstances because it is from Him.

Read Philippians 1:1-30

Paul and Timothy, servants of Christ Jesus, To all God's holy people in Christ Jesus at Philippi, together with the overseers and deacons; Grace and peace to you from God our Father and the Lord Jesus Christ. I thank my God every time I remember you. In all my prayers for all of you, I always pray with joy because of your partnership in the gospel from the first day until now, being confident of this, that he who began a good work in you will carry it on to completion until the day of Christ Jesus. It is right for me to feel this way about all of you, since I have you in my heart and, whether I am in chains or defending and confirming the gospel, all of you share in God's grace with me. God can testify how I long for all of you with the affection of Christ Jesus. And this is my prayer: that your love may abound more and more in knowledge and depth of insight, so that you may be able to discern what is best and may be pure and blameless for the day of Christ, filled with the fruit of righteousness that comes through Jesus Christ—to the glory and praise of God. Now I want you to know, brothers and sisters, that what has happened to me has actually served to advance the gospel. As a result, it has become clear throughout the whole palace guard and to everyone else that I am in chains for Christ. And because of my chains, most of the brothers and sisters have become confident in the Lord and dare all the more to proclaim the gospel without fear. It is true that some preach Christ out of envy and rivalry, but others out of goodwill. The latter do so out of love, knowing that I am put here for the defense of the gospel. The former preach Christ out of selfish ambition, not sincerely, supposing that they can stir up trouble for me while I am in chains. But what does it matter? The important thing is that in every way, whether from false motives or true, Christ is preached. And because of this I rejoice. Yes, and I will continue to rejoice, for

I know that through your prayers and God's provision of the Spirit of Jesus Christ what has happened to me will turn out for my deliverance. I eagerly expect and hope that I will in no way be ashamed, but will have sufficient courage so that now as always Christ will be exalted in my body, whether by life or by death. For to me, to live is Christ and to die is gain. If I am to go on living in the body, this will mean fruitful labor for me. Yet what shall I choose? I do not know! I am torn between the two: I desire to depart and be with Christ, which is better by far; but it is more necessary for you that I remain in the body. Convinced of this, I know that I will remain, and I will continue with all of you for your progress and joy in the faith, so that through my being with you again your boasting in Christ Jesus will abound on account of me. Whatever happens, conduct yourselves in a manner worthy of the gospel of Christ. Then, whether I come and see you or only hear about you in my absence, I will know that you stand firm in the one Spirit, striving together as one for the faith of the gospel without being frightened in any way by those who oppose you. This is a sign to them that they will be destroyed, but that you will be saved—and that by God. For it has been granted to you on behalf of Christ not only to believe in him, but also to suffer for him, since you are going through the same struggle you saw I had, and now hear that I still have.

Paul, an amazing leader, follower and teacher of God's word, shared in Philippians about being happy in Christ because of his joy in Christ. Paul was writing a note of encouragement and affirmation while in prison to the church in Philippi that he had started. Here are some valuable lessons he is teaching us about joy.

Joy results in thankfulness. When you are filled with God's Holy Spirit because you have accepted Christ into your heart and are saved, you will begin to experience true and lasting joy. You begin to see this life and all its ups and downs as something to be thankful for. Paul, in his grim circumstances, starts by saying how much he thanks God for them. Joy from God can't help but result in an attitude of gratefulness. This thankfulness allows you to have joy in all situations.

Q: What you thankful for today?

Joy comes from a life of prayer. Paul shares how he prays with joy. As you pray, growing your relationship with God, God will show you how to be joyful in all situations. As you practice being joyful, adjusting your attitude, allowing God to show you what He is doing, you will move into a place of such peace. Your prayer life will get better. You will see the changes that are being made in others, including yourself.

Q: Share about your prayer life. Could it improve? What needs changing?

Joy comes from being Christ-focused first and as a result, other-focused. As we focus on our relationship with God, seeking Him first, we will want to focus on bringing others to Him. How powerful! You can just feel Paul's joy because he knows he is not alone. Jesus never meant for us to journey alone. There are others that also understand the purpose of life. Do you remember the acronym you learned when you were a child? J=Jesus, O=Others, Y=Yourself. Maybe it's time to put JOY up on the wall again.

Q: Who are those in your life that share your desire to be other-focused?

Joy is the same in all situations. Paul shares how even in chains, in a dirty, smelly, prison, he is joyful because he knows the reason he is there. We need to look at our lives, praying for God to manifest His joy in all situations so that we can smile even in pain, in hurt, in brokenness, and in the unknown. This means that even if we have some temporary happiness in our lives, the experience does not consume us—the joy is what consumes us!

Q: Do you believe you have the power to be like Paul? Why or why not?

Joy is permanent. Once you have accepted Christ, joy stays with you. But we need encouragement to keep going in tough times. We need to be reminded that God has called, anointed, appointed, and equipped us to do HIS work. And

His work will not be over until Christ comes back. Amazing... this work, this journey, this path is His path. Because I am doing what God has asked me to do, I can have the everlasting joy. Joy that will never go away. It's not temporary or based on circumstances. Joy that is forever and eternal.

Q: When did you accept Christ as your Savior? Share.

WHAT ARE YOU GOING TO WALK AWAY WITH?
What is God saying to you right now?

[Close in prayer; option to list prayer requests here so you can pray through the week for each other.]

ASSIGNMENT:

As you walk with the Lord, knowing what joy really is, you will begin to look at "being happy" differently. You will begin to see that although the new pair of jeans makes you happy for now, the feeling is temporary. You will then seek to find things that bring you lasting joy—like hearing a child laugh, helping an elderly person carry their groceries to the car, seeing a rainbow after a horrible storm, or paying for the next person's bill in line at Starbucks. This kind of joy comes from God. It becomes about Him and not about you.

1. Pray and ask God to show you the things, the people, the situations that illustrate the "happiness versus joy" concept.

2. Pray and ask God to grow your joy: letting go of your focus on things that are temporarily making you happy.

3. Read and memorize Psalm 68:3
But may the righteous be glad and rejoice before God; may they be happy and joyful.

Chapter 3:
Walk the Line:
Loneliness versus Alone-ness

Lord, Why Have You Left Me Alone?

"Why, Lord? Why am I still single? Why have you left me alone? I am so lonely. I can't stand it. I hate always being by myself. I simply hate it."

Loneliness comes up as the number one thing that Christians who are single complain about on the many polls completed through the Singles Network Ministries. This is especially the case if the person was once married, ending a dating relationship, or if they had kids who are no longer living at home. That loss of company in their life has caused such emptiness, making it hard to function sometimes. The loneliness seems to overpower any sense of wisdom on their part and can even lead some people to make bad choices for friendships, dating relationships, and eventually marriage partners. They would rather put any person in their life (whether from God or not), than to feel lonely.

Personally, until my dad's death, I had never experienced utter loneliness. Sure, I had been alone and would miss friends and family sometimes. However, this sense of hopelessness was something that I had never experienced as a Christian. My dad had been sick for many years with Alzheimer's. I had the honor of moving in with my parents during the last nine months of his life to help take care of him. He left this earth and went into the arms of the Lord. For the next year after his death, I would find myself lying on the couch, in a state of depression and deep hopelessness.

So, why would I feel any loneliness? Why would I feel so hopeless? Well, the loss of a family member, friend, or spouse by death or distance, loss of a career, or loss of anything significant can lead to these emotions. The loneliness and hopelessness are not based on God's truth. For a Christian, these emotions can be sinful, and can be something the enemy uses to attack us. The loss of my dad left me alone but not lonely.

Feeling lonely is:

Feeling alone is:

The Fine Line Revealed:

As a Christian, when you say you are lonely it may be because you are, in fact, alone. Being alone is a real place we sometimes find ourselves in, whereas, being lonely is something a person experiences. To say, "I feel alone" is being honest, because in some cases we are, and it isn't much fun.

Jesus felt alone many times in various ways. He understands what it feels like to have the whole world on your shoulders, with no one to help you carry the load. Even though Jesus had twelve disciples who were there to help Him, they would abandon Him over and over.

Read Luke 22:4-6
And Judas went to the chief priests and the officers of the temple guard and discussed with them how he might betray Jesus. They were delighted and agreed to give him money. He consented, and watched for an opportunity to hand Jesus over to them when no crowd was present.

Judas would betray him.
Many of you know what it feels like to betrayed—to have that one person you cared about the most lie to you. Maybe it was an ex-spouse, business partner, or friend who betrayed you. They were smiling to your face while at the same time being dishonest with you. Losing trust may cause you to feel lonely.

Q: Who has betrayed you? Share.

Q: How does it make you feel to read about Judas and what he did?

Read Matthew 26:34

"I tell you the truth," Jesus answered, "this very night, before the rooster crows, you will disown Me three times."

Peter would deny him.

Maybe you got into a situation where you needed your friends to be there. You needed the support of your family, only to have them deny you. Friends who said they had your back but when things got really tough, the phone calls went unanswered and emails bounced back. Peter would deny Jesus, even though he had promised to stand by Him.

Q: Have you ever been in a situation like Peter where you denied Christ? What about a time you didn't share your faith when God asked you to?

Q: Share a time when you were disowned, forgotten, or rejected? How did it feel?

Q: How do you think Christ felt when Peter abandoned him? What about when we abandon Christ?

Read Luke 22:45-46
When He rose from prayer and went back to the disciples, He found them asleep, exhausted from sorrow. "Why are you sleeping?" He asked them. "Get up and pray so that you will not fall into temptation."

Jesus's disciples would fail him.

How many of you have had folks let you down? Maybe you led a team at your company or your church, only to have your teammates fail to follow through on an important project. Some people might have quit, causing more work for you. Even Jesus could not escape those who would fail to help Him in His hour of need.

Q: Why did Jesus tell the disciples to pray?

Q: How often are you tempted to do things you know is wrong? Share some of those things.

Read John 19:25-27
Near the cross of Jesus stood His mother, His mother's sister, Mary the wife of Clopas, and Mary Magdalene. When Jesus saw His mother there, and the disciple whom He loved standing nearby, He said to His mother, "Dear woman, here is your son," and to the disciple, "Here is your mother." From that time on, this disciple took her into his home.

Jesus's disciples would abandon Him.
Your former spouse said you would be together until death do you part, but "death" of the marriage turned out to occur five or ten years after you both said "I do." Maybe a parent abandoned you as a child or withheld support from you as you grew older. Perhaps the child you raised, loved, cried and worried over has abandoned you. They may return in the future like the prodigal son, but in the meantime, it feels horrible to experience rejection after having loved your child so unconditionally.

Jesus understands abandonment. When Jesus was hanging on the cross, only one disciple showed up: John. Where were the other men He spent the last three years, day and night, 24/7 with? The ones whom He taught, encouraged, and trained to take over for Him? If Jesus, who is perfect, would have His closest friends abandon Him, then surely we are going to have people abandon us. The issue is not if it's going to happen, but when—and how do we handle it?

Jesus focused on the present, asking His best friend and mother to care for each other. He focused on Mary Magdalene and Mary, wife of Clopas. Mary Magdalene would be the first to see that Christ had risen from the dead; the first "evangelist" so to speak. Although most of His disciples did abandon Him at the cross, they would not abandon Him afterwards. His teaching, His love for them, His example would come through in the end. So yet, again, Jesus is showing us that through the things that would cause most people to feel lonely and hopeless, they are in fact merely causing us to feel alone. But Jesus had God and so do we. We have a choice in how we live through these situations. We have a choice in how we use circumstances to bring glory to God.

Q: Why do you think the disciples abandoned Christ at the cross?

Q: What kind of relationship did John and Mary Magdalene have with Jesus that was different than the other followers?

Q: When we trust Christ as our Savior, we are given responsibility. As we grow, as we are obedient, this responsibility increases. Mary Magdalene, Jesus's mother, and John would be given more to do after Jesus's death; what is Jesus asking of you?

Read Deuteronomy 31:6
Be strong and courageous. Do not be afraid or terrified because of them, for the LORD your God goes with you; he will never leave you nor forsake you.

We are not truly alone.

Jesus reminds us: "Come to me, all you who are weary and burdened, and I will give you rest." (Matthew 11:28). This should give us comfort when we are trying to carry burdens such as kids, a home, finances, elderly parents, or work. Here is a cool thing: when you know the Lord as your Savior, you are never truly alone or forsaken. God is always with us, giving us comfort, encouragement, and hope.

God is still there, despite what the world does to us, despite betrayal and abandonment by humans, He has not moved or changed. Doesn't that make you smile? Doesn't that make you rejoice? The lost are lonely because they are alone in every sense. There is no comfort from the Holy Spirit and, no hope of an everlasting life in Christ. All the more reason we have to keep our focus on reaching the lost versus feeling discouraged about ourselves.

Q: How does knowing that you are not alone, that God is with you, make you feel?

So then, for those that are not married, why are we physically alone? Why hasn't God brought me someone?

First, sometimes we are physically alone because that seems to be the only time God can get our attention. When we are alone (the kids are gone, the house is empty, work is done) and all we have is silence and God, we are forced to talk (and listen) to God. The problem is that most of us do whatever we can to avoid this quiet alone-ness. We watch TV, talk on the phone, play on facebook, eat, shop, and whatever else we can do to avoid talking with Jesus. We avoid having to hear Him say that this is where we are going to be for now. But in avoiding seeking God in the alone-ness, we are also avoiding hearing God say He is with us. We avoid all the plans He wants to share with us. We avoid all the things He wants to tell us that will help us in this journey as single adults. God wants to empower, encourage, and equip us. Our "alone" times should be precious and valued.

So, why hasn't God brought someone to help fill in these "alone" times? Well, you have asked the million-dollar question. I simply do not have the answer you seek. I just know God is still in charge and knows best. For me, it doesn't appear getting married has been a part of His plan up to this point. But thank God, because of my singleness, I have been able to encourage so many others to live full and complete lives without being married. I have been able to write, speak, and teach all over the USA and abroad, imparting that our only hope is found in Christ. When the enemy whispers, "You are so lonely, no one will ever want you," you will have the knowledge and strength to rebuke the enemy because you know the truth. You do have hope, and even though right now you are physically alone, you do have a relationship with Christ.

Q: As a married person or a single person, when has being alone physically been a good thing? What has God revealed?

WHAT ARE YOU GOING TO WALK AWAY WITH?
What is God saying to you right now?

[Close in prayer; option to list prayer requests here so you can pray through the week for each other.]

ASSIGNMENT:

1. Spend more time "alone" with God, allowing Him to speak into your life. Go to the next level in trusting Him for all things.

2. Start journaling what God is saying to you about this area.

3. Pray for someone you can help who is feeling lonely because they do not have the hope of Jesus Christ in their lives. Spend some time with them, share your faith, encourage them and allow God to lead them to Christ or be encouraged in Christ.

Chapter 4:
Walk the Line: Gossip versus Venting

"My Pastor Drives Me Crazy"

"Lord, here I am again ...in yet another church that doesn't seem to care that I am single. Sure, they take my tithes, ask me to help watch the zillion kids in childcare, but they mostly ignore me. I just hate it. I hate being forgotten. I hate that my pastor never addresses singleness from the pulpit. I am not even sure if he knows who I am, much less that I am single. And our deacons, are you sure they are even breathing? What about the committees of this church? It seems like you can't change a light bulb without a committee to decide when to change it. And another thing...."

You know, the comments from this single person sound a lot like I use to sound when I was much younger. But it also sounds like a lot of people I know that are married, too. The bottom-line is we all go to churches where there are things we do not like. Maybe it's the pastor's last sermon, how they spend the mission's money, or how they involved you (or didn't).

But maybe it's more than just your church that bugs you. Maybe you also have some complaints about your job. Maybe your boss drives you nuts—he keeps you overtime without any concern that you might have a life. Or maybe it's a neighbor who constantly plays loud music or never cuts the grass. Or maybe it's a friend who constantly dates the wrong girl/guy and never seems to get it.

How do most people handle their complaints? They tell others. You may have heard the old saying, "if you love a restaurant, you tell two or three people, but if you are unhappy, you tell an army." The problem with "telling an army" is that what may be a simple complaint or a time of venting becomes gossip. This gossip cannot only spread, it can cause pain to others, even destroy relationships. It can also cause damage to a person's reputation, even in their church or workplace. We all get frustrated—it's how you handle the frustration that makes the difference. The ripples from words of discord spread wide.

I know this because I have experienced first-hand the consequences of having a person vent to me over the years about the church they attended. I was told about every person who was there, what they said in Sunday school, and how they reacted to various things. I was also told anything the pastor said or did, if it was wrong in the eyes of my friend. From time to time I would point out that these complaints sounded like gossip. My friend said it was just "venting" and that my friend needed to tell me this stuff to help deal with it. I would visit this church from time to time, and as a result of years of hearing only negatives, I began to draw opinions about the various people there. People that I used to like.

Read Matthew 12:36
But I tell you that everyone will have to give account on the day of judgment for every empty word they have spoken.

So, what is the difference between gossip and venting? What is the fine line?

Venting is:

Gossip is:

GOSSIP

Gossip can sometimes appear as "sharing someone's prayer request" or "venting" when in reality a part of your heart is hoping that what you are saying will make you look better and another person look worse. You say these things not only to feel better about who you are, but also to feel better about what you do. You are not really concerned with the outcome. You ask people not to say anything but you know deep down inside, they might. Gossip is very self-focused.

Gossip is also something I find people do when they struggle with self-esteem, and with being a people pleaser. When you start to tell someone about your church, your boss, or your friend—ask yourself what type of things are you sharing and why? Are you sharing a character flaw? Are you sharing a sin? Are you sharing something they did wrong to you? What is your ultimate goal in talking about them behind their backs? And to whom are you talking about them? Are you really sharing because they need prayer?

Q: When at times have you gossiped and why?

Q: Why do you think people gossip?

Q: When have you been the victim of gossip? What did you do about it?

Read Exodus 23:1
Do not spread false reports. Do not help a guilty person by being a malicious witness.

Read Leviticus 19:16
"'Do not go about spreading slander among your people. Do not do anything that endangers your neighbor's life. I am the Lord.'"

Q: How can gossip endanger a person's life or help a guilty person?

VENTING:
We all have times when we need to vent. We simply need to share about things that are frustrating us, be it church, school, or friends. Venting allows us to hear our own voice, hear the problem, and even work it out. Venting allows us to process the stress. People who vent may or may not be looking for a solution. Sometimes, they know God has placed them in a specific situation: amongst those aggravating people at work, on a committee at church, or next door to a particular neighbor. They know that God is using them to reach those people. When we hear someone vent, the frustration we hear is usually just a release of stress about the situation. Everyone listening knows there will be some kind of victory in the end.

You can even set up your venting to say: I love my pastor but sometimes he frustrates me when he...or I love my friend but when she does this, it hurts me. Venting is other-focused.

Q: Share some examples of when you have had to vent? Who have you vented to and why?

Read Ephesians 4:29
Do not let any unwholesome talk come out of your mouths, but only what is helpful for building others up according to their needs, that it may benefit those who listen.

Q: What has resulted in your venting about something or someone?

Read James 1: 26
Those who consider themselves religious and yet do not keep a tight rein on their tongues deceive themselves, and their religion is worthless.

Read Proverbs 11:13
A gossip betrays a confidence, but a trustworthy person keeps a secret.

Q: Why is controlling our tongues so important to our witness?

The Fine Line Revealed:

In order to know where the fine line is the next time you want to share, make sure you:

Read Proverbs 19:20
Listen to advice and accept discipline, and at the end you will be counted among the wise.

1. Vent to those who know you well and that you consider to be strong, wise counsel. Find those people that are willing to speak truth into your life and stop you if they know what you are saying is really gossip.

Q: Who in your life do you consider wise counsel?

Read 1 Timothy 5:13-14
(in reference to young widows who are distracted from their focus on God)

Besides, they get into the habit of being idle and going about from house to house. And not only do they become idlers, but also busybodies who talk nonsense, saying things they ought not to. So, I counsel younger widows to marry, to have children, to manage their homes and to give the enemy no opportunity for slander.

2. Vent with the openness to allow the Holy Spirit to make changes in you and in those with whom you are frustrated and also offer the other person an opportunity to suggest direction.

Q: What type of advice is Timothy sharing here?

Read Philippians 4:6
Do not be anxious about anything, but in every situation, by prayer and petition, with thanksgiving, present your requests to God.

3. Pray before speaking about anything that you think someone else needs to hear. Ask yourself, "why do I feel the need to say something? OK, so my Sunday school teacher taught something wrong in the Bible. Do I tell everyone I know what they taught was a mistake OR do I ask to set up an appointment and ask for clarity of what they said?" Your friend is a huge flirt with all the men. Do you tell everyone she is a flirt or again, confront her in love to share this? I realize not every aggravating situation is solved by just talking to the person. Some of us have situations we are in that we are not always able to do anything about.

Q: Have you ever wanted to talk about something that bothered you but held back from speaking, at least until you prayed about it? Share.

WHAT ARE YOU GOING TO WALK AWAY WITH? What is God saying to you right now?

[Close in prayer; option to list prayer requests here so you can pray through the week for each other.]

ASSIGNMENT:
When faced with a negative situation:

1) Pray, allowing God to reveal what He is trying to do through it.

2) Become the solution instead of the problem. Pray about where God would have you get involved, helping to make some positive changes.

For example: If you don't like some of the ways that things are being done at church, then ask how you can be involved to help make changes. If you don't like your neighbor's long grass, offer to mow it for them. If you don't like your cubicle mate's voice, put on headphones. But seriously, seek a way to solve the problem where you build a bridge instead of destroying it. Remember, as a believer you are the light, you are Christ's example. How you react, what you say and/or do will reflect your relationship with Christ.

Read Ephesians 4:11-13
So Christ Himself gave some as the apostles, the prophets, the evangelists, the pastors and teachers, to equip His people for works of service, so that the body of Christ may be built up until we all reach unity in the faith and in the knowledge of the Son of God and become mature, attaining to the whole measure of the fullness of Christ.

3) Remember that some things we think or see should be kept to ourselves. Remember the greatest commandment.

Read Matthew 22:37-40
Jesus replied: "'Love the Lord your God with all your heart and with all your soul and with all your mind.' This is the first and greatest commandment. And the second is like it: 'Love your neighbor as yourself.' All the Law and the Prophets hang on these two commandments."

Q: Pray and ask God who you can love today, despite what you may think about them?

Chapter 5:
Walk the Line: Lust versus Love

What's Love Got to Do With It?

Why does he have to take off his shirt yet again? Doesn't he know that women are gawking at him? Doesn't he know that all that skin is making some of us uncomfortable? That some of us are thinking thoughts that are...well, you get the idea (I have got to stop watching those butter commercials).

Yep, a butter commercial. Or how about milkshakes? Or better yet, dusting spray. It seems no matter when you turn on the TV, there is someone trying to sell you something using sex to get your attention. Years ago, I got so tired of all the horrible commercials and TV shows and movies that I cut the cord to my TV three times only to rewire it later. Eventually, I just got rid of my TV and chose not to watch it for five years. Sure, I watched it in hotels and with my friends and family—but in my own home, I had a problem. Without the accountability of a roommate, spouse or kids, there was just too much that was taking me down the road of lust, which often turned my thoughts to sex. Some of these shows and commercials that seem innocent were actually attacking my mind through my eyes, my ears, and my mouth. Where were the TV shows about caring for others without anything in return? Where were the commercial messages that said "love your neighbor," not try to jump on them? And due to this constant attack from our TVs (and other media outlets), how is anyone to know the difference? Where is the fine line?

Lust is:

Love is:

LUST:
Lust is always self-focused. When we lust, we are in a battle of seeking only to pleasure ourselves. We can lust not only for things of a sexual nature but also for jobs, money, power, or relationships. We can become so self-focused in our attempts to get these things that we are blinded to the journey...the journey towards death. Because this world will never satisfy you, you will NEVER get enough. Something that starts as innocently as buying a few pairs of shoes can turn into maxing out your credit card, looking at a porn magazine can escalate into watching it on the computer, or reading one romance novel can lead to joining an addicts club, and lust has taken over. Lust will begin to feed on your self-focused desires. You will find yourself talking others into becoming a part of your destructive journey as well. If someone is also committing the same sin, at least you are not alone. But eventually, lust will tear down your relationships, too, and you will BE ALONE.

Q: What are some areas of your life in which you have lusted? Share.

Q: How does our lust affect others?

LOVE:
Love is other-focused. When we love—our goals, our purpose, our desires are to please the other person. Whether it's helping someone with their yard work, serving at church, taking a grocery cart back to the store for someone, or dating/marrying with respect and honor, all these actions are other-focused. When you love someone, you will want the best for him or her. You will want to lift them toward Christ. You will want to build a bridge, not tear it down. When you love another person, you are not thinking of what you are going to get out of it but how God gets the glory. Love does not go too far sexually, yell at you, intentionally hurt you, lie, or cheat. If you have pure love, in all things you will want to

show the love that Christ has shown to you. Love leads to relationships and NOT BEING ALONE.

Q: Share a small act of love you have witnessed in the last week.

Q: Share a story of what you have seen as real love between friends, family, someone you have dated or married.

The Fine Line Revealed:

In order to identify the fine line of lust vs. love:

Read 1 John 2:16
For everything in the world—the cravings of sinful man, the lust of his eyes and the boasting of what he has and does— comes not from the Father but from the world.

When you are watching TV, reading a book, or going to a movie, ask yourself, "Is what I am watching or reading lifting Christ up or pulling Him (and me) down?" Remember, what we see and absorb can become who we are. We have a tendency to lust because of the things we are seeing and reading. It's the way the enemy gets us.

Q: Why do we lust?

Q: How does lust tear us down?

Read Ezekiel 6:9
Then in the nations where they have been carried captive, those who escape will remember me—how I have been grieved by their adulterous hearts, which have turned away from me, and by their eyes, which have lusted after their idols. They will loathe themselves for the evil they have done and for all their detestable practices.

Q: How does lusting tear down our relationship with the Father?

Read Matthew 5:28
But I tell you that anyone who looks at a woman lustfully has already committed adultery with her in his heart.

God says lust in our eyes is the same as adultery with our bodies. God takes this very seriously...do you? And remember folks, it's also our responsibility to dress appropriately and behave modestly so that we aren't part of the problem.

Q: When you look upon the opposite sex, do you allow your mind to wander? What are some methods you have used to help you avoid falling into the temptation of lust?

Read Job 31:1
I made a covenant with my eyes not to look lustfully at a girl.

Read Matthew 6:33
But seek first his kingdom and his righteousness, and all these things will be given to you as well.

Q: What is a covenant?

Q: Do you have friends who can hold you accountable with your struggles of lust? Are you praying about your struggles, seeking Christ in all things? Share.

Bottom-line, in lusting, one will always seek to please oneself, building your own kingdom instead of God's Kingdom. Start working toward God's Kingdom today by asking God to help you. Start serving in your church or community. Only when we help others, when we see the pain and brokenness, can we break the bondage and slavery caused by lust. Remember to love, because God is love. Start using your eyes and ears to hear and see God so you can love and be loved by Him. As it is written, "No eye has seen, no ear has heard, no mind has conceived what God has prepared for those who love Him." (1 Corinthians 2:9)

WHAT ARE YOU GOING TO WALK AWAY WITH? What is God saying to you right now?

[Close in prayer; option to list prayer requests here so you can pray through the week for each other.]

ASSIGNMENT:
1. Pray and ask God to reveal areas of lust that you need to surrender to Him.

2. Pray about who can be your accountability partner (and ask him/her) to help you resist the temptation to return to lusting for those things. Be willing to get professional help if needed.

Chapter 6:
Walk the Line: Doubt versus Questioning God

What do you mean?

"God, why do You allow me to be in this place? Things are going so well and then bam, catastrophe! Lord, why would You allow this to happen? I am dating this great guy, things seem to be going well... and then he breaks up with me. Why would you let my heart be broken like that? Also, Lord, every time I save up just a bit of money, something breaks in my house. And my job, Lord, is this all there is in life? Get up, go to work, come home, eat, go to bed, and then do it all over again? God, are You there? Are You listening? Do You really care at all?"

Does any of this sound familiar to you? Maybe your crisis of belief occurs more frequently when dealing with your kids, your ex, or your extended family. Maybe you doubt God when you don't feel His presence every day. Maybe you have asked God to heal you from cancer, diabetes, or a broken relationship. Or maybe you just simply feel alone and you aren't sure if God is out there.

Note: This chapter is not about whether or not you believe there is a God. It's about knowing there is a difference between doubting who God is versus questioning what He does.

Doubting God is:

Questioning God is:

DOUBTING:
A feeling of uncertainty or lack of conviction. Depending on your maturity in Christ, we can often doubt God. We might question what He is doing in our lives. We see things happen around us and we can get so blinded by the enemy. We don't see how God is going to help us out of the situation. We simply settle on man's best versus God's best. Because God doesn't work on our timetable, we lose our trust in Him. When we doubt, we become very self-focused. You forget how God has come through in so many other situations in your life, and question whether He is going to come through in the future. We doubt God when we truly do not believe who He says He is. We have to learn to trust God, to be obedient, no matter what. Please understand, if God has appointed you, He has then anointed you. He will equip you and always provide. This is God's process with His children, His heirs. Because of this truth, we have no need to ever doubt. Doubt comes from the enemy, not from God, whereas questioning can be from God.

Read James 1:5-8
If any of you lacks wisdom, you should ask God, who gives generously to all without finding fault, and it will be given to you. But when you ask, you must believe and not doubt, because the one who doubts is like a wave of the sea, blown and tossed by the wind. That person should not expect to receive anything from the Lord. Such a person is double-minded and unstable in all they do.

Q: How can doubt make you like a wave of the sea, blown and tossed about by the wind?

QUESTIONING GOD:
When we question God, we aren't saying that we don't believe due to our limitation, we are saying we want more information. It's OK to question God as long as our motivation is not about us but about seeking God's will. We don't question God to say we think He is making the wrong decision. We are questioning God to help us understand the situation. We are asking God for more details and a clearer direction. When we do question God, we can let Him know we are frustrated and upset. Even David cried out to God with anger. We can tell God what we like and don't like about the situation. We can even tell Him we are afraid. But the bottom-line is that we have to come to that place of trust. God chooses to reveal what He wants, when He wants. Asking God keeps us in a balanced relationship with God, whereas doubting keeps things one-sided.

Read Deuteronomy 29:29
The secret things belong to the LORD our God, but the things revealed belong to us and to our children forever, that we may follow all the words of this law.

Q: How does God reveal Himself to you?

The Fine Line Revealed:

In order to know where the fine line is for doubting versus questioning God, the Bible gives us numerous examples of people who also doubted and questioned God. Spend some time reading their stories. See if you can pick out the differences.

Nicodemus

Read John 3:4
"How can someone be born when they are old?" Nicodemus asked. "Surely they cannot enter a second time into their mother's womb to be born!"

Q: What was the message God was trying to teach to Nicodemus?

Q: Was Nicodemus doubting or questioning God?

Moses

Read Exodus 6:12
But Moses said to the LORD, "If the Israelites will not listen to me, why would Pharaoh listen to me, since I speak with faltering lips?"

Read Exodus 19:9
The LORD said to Moses, "I am going to come to you in a dense cloud, so that the people will hear me speaking with you and will always put their trust in you." Then Moses told the LORD what the people had said.

Q: Like Moses, how have you doubted God in who you are or where He has called you to go or what He has called you to do?

Q: Was Moses doubting or questioning God?

Thomas

Read John 20:27
Then he said to Thomas, "Put your finger here; see my hands. Reach out your hand and put it into my side. Stop doubting and believe."

Q: When has God asked you to totally trust Him? What did He do to get you to that point?

Q: Was Thomas doubting or questioning God?

Zechariah

Read Luke 1: 18
Zechariah asked the angel, "How can I be sure of this? I am an old man and my wife is well along in years."

Q: What do you have a hard time believing about God's Word?

Q: Was Zechariah doubting or questioning God?

Gideon

Read Judges 6:13
"Pardon me, my lord," Gideon replied, "but if the Lord is with us, why has all this happened to us? Where are all his wonders that our ancestors told us about when they said, 'Did not the LORD bring us up out of Egypt?' But now the LORD has abandoned us and given us into the hand of Midian."

Q: Like Gideon, have you ever felt abandoned by God? Share.

Q: Was Gideon doubting or questioning God?

Mary, Mother of Jesus

Read Luke 1:34
"How will this be," Mary asked the angel, "since I am a virgin?"

Q: What do you think Mary was thinking when she asked this? Has God ever told you something that didn't seem possible to believe?

Q: Was Mary doubting or questioning God?

Bottom-line, we all have times when we question God, even doubt. We can easily get fixed on the limits of this world and forget about the unlimited world of God. For myself, I often start to question God when my provision isn't where I would like it to be. I question God on speaking events, the audience, and work issues. But every time, God comes through. He reminds me of how special we all are. He reminds me to trust Him. He reminds me that He loves us. And that all is for our good, and for His glory.

"For My thoughts are not your thoughts, neither are your ways My ways," declares the LORD. (Isaiah 55:8).

WHAT ARE YOU GOING TO WALK AWAY WITH? What is God saying to you right now?

[Close in prayer; option to list prayer requests here so you can pray through the week for each other.]

ASSIGNMENT:
1. Pray and ask God to reveal areas of your life that you struggle with in relation to doubt.

2. Pray and ask God for a mentor, someone who knows more about the Bible than you, who can help you increase your Biblical knowledge (to understand those things that you might not be sure about).

3. Pray and ask God to show you His truths in all things, including binding the enemy from his attacks and lies.

Chapter 7:
Walk the Line: Worry versus Concern

You're Such a Worry Wart

When I was a little girl, I spent a lot of time at my grandma Bell's home. She was always very busy, whether in the fields gathering fresh vegetables and fruits, standing over her stove cooking, or cleaning her house. She rarely sat down unless she was shucking corn or snapping green beans. We all got to enjoy her made-from-scratch meals such as chicken and dumplings, buttered corn on the cob, and fresh peaches over homemade ice cream. Mmmm, good.

As I look back on those days I can say with all honesty that I never once heard my grandmother complain or be worried about her life. She had more to be worried about than most of us. She married my grandfather who already had seven children, and then they had five more kids. They raised their children on a small farm. So if the weather was bad, their entire crop could have gone under. As the years passed, my grandmother would end up taking care of my aunt who died at age 31 of multiple sclerosis, and then my grandfather who couldn't walk. And yet, she never complained. One day, when I was in my twenties, I asked grandma if she ever worried about her life. She said, "Worrying is like a rocking chair. It doesn't get you anywhere but it gives you something to do." I had to think about it. She went on to say, she "didn't have time to worry because there was too much to get done." I replied "So grandma, you never got concerned about things?" She went on to say, "Now don't get worried mixed up with being concerned. You can't have 12 kids, be poor and not be concerned." Where is the fine line that divides worry from concern?

Worry is:

Concern is:

WORRY:
Worrying is a state of mind where you are anxious about something. This anxiety can be severe at times to the point of obsession. You go over and over in your mind what the problem may be and how to fix it. Most of the time, you are not able to fix things because they are out of your control. This obsession can lead to stress. This stress can lead to mental, physical, and even spiritual issues. When you worry about anything in this way, you are not trusting God. Your focus becomes on the problem instead of the Lord as the solution and it is easy to forget who is really in control.

CONCERN

Concern can sometimes look like worry. It all depends on the perspective and the goal of the concerned party. When you are concerned over a situation, you are simply exhibiting care. You care about your children coming home too late. You care about your work, your health, and your relationships. Because you know you can't control the situation, you must trust God to handle things for you. Being concerned is being responsible. Being concerned turns you towards Christ for help, for prayer, and for a solution.

The Fine Line Revealed:

Don't Worry, God Knows What You Need

God reminds us how valuable we are to Him. So if we know this, then why do we worry so much about everything? Worrying will not add one more minute to our lives. This is why we need to trust Him for all things.

Read Matthew 6:25-34
"Therefore I tell you, do not worry about your life, what you will eat or drink; or about your body, what you will wear. Is not life more than food, and the body more than clothes? Look at the birds of the air; they do not sow or reap or store away in barns, and yet your heavenly Father feeds them. Are you not much more valuable than they? Can any one of you by worrying add a single hour to your life? "And why do you worry about clothes? See how the flowers of the field grow. They do not labor or spin. Yet I tell you that not even Solomon in all his splendor was dressed like one of these. If that is how God clothes the grass of the field, which is here today and tomorrow is thrown into the fire, will he not much more clothe you—you of little faith? So do not worry, saying, 'What shall we eat?' or 'What shall we drink?' or 'What shall we wear?' For the pagans run after all these things, and your heavenly Father knows that you need them. But seek first his kingdom and his righteousness, and all these things will be given to you as well. Therefore do not worry about tomorrow, for tomorrow will worry about itself. Each day has enough trouble of its own."

Q: What are the things in your life that you seem to worry about, versus just being concerned?

Q: When has God shown you His care and provision beyond what you expected?

Don't Worry, God Will Speak For You

Most of us have a hard time witnessing to others. We are so afraid of rejection. What if they ask you something you don't know? What if you say something that could get you into trouble? No matter what, remember, the Holy Spirit is always available to do the speaking for you. You just have to allow Him.

Read Matthew 10:19-20

But when they arrest you, do not worry about what to say or how to say it. At that time you will be given what to say, for it will not be you speaking, but the Spirit of your Father speaking through you.

Q: Do you have an easy or hard time sharing your faith?

Q: What are some ways you share with others about how to witness without worry?

But Be Aware, Worry Can Distract

Like Martha, how quickly things in our lives like TVs, cell phones, sports, work, and relationships distract us from Christ.

Read Luke 10: 41-42

"Martha, Martha," the Lord answered, "you are worried and upset about many things, but few things are needed—or indeed only one. Mary has chosen what is better, and it will not be taken away from her."

Q: What things in your life distract you the most?

Q: How has your relationship with the Lord been affected by this?

Do Be Concerned as it Leads to Trust

Abraham would take his son and out of obedience prepare him to be sacrificed to the Lord. Abraham would not worry but trust God to provide what was necessary. God asks the same from us. He wants our time, our service, and our tithes. He wants us to trust Him to provide even when we do not see how He is going to do it.

Read Genesis 21:11-12

The matter distressed Abraham greatly because it concerned his son. But God said to him, "Do not be so distressed about the boy and your slave woman. Listen to whatever Sarah tells you, because it is through Isaac that your offspring will be reckoned."

Q: What is God asking you to be concerned about right now in relation to trusting Him?

Do Be Concerned But Put Christ First

Our concerns, even with the best intentions, can become about us. God instructs us to make sure all of our concerns have Him in mind first. So when you are praying about your job, your sickness, your kids, your friends, your boyfriend/girlfriend, etc., you need to ask God what He wants.

Read Matthew 16:23

Jesus turned and said to Peter, "Get behind me, Satan! You are a stumbling block to me; you do not have in mind the concerns of God, but merely human concerns."

Q: Do you really believe God has you? That He has what is best for you? Then do you pray believing this? Do you pray, submitting your whole life and direction to Him? Share.

Bottom-line, we can all too easily become worried about our lives. It's hard to trust God in all things. God may not do things the way we want. God may not give us an answer at the time we want. But seriously, when has worrying added anything to your life? When has worrying changed the situation? So yes, be concerned. But let that concern turn you towards the Lord in prayer, trusting in God's answers to come when and how He chooses. Then, let others see how you handle the tough situations of life. Be the witness who doesn't worry but trusts the Lord in all things.

Read Proverbs 3:5-6
Trust in the LORD with all your heart and lean not on your own understanding; in all your ways submit to him, and he will make your paths straight.

WHAT ARE YOU GOING TO WALK AWAY WITH?
What is God saying to you right now?

[Close in prayer; option to list prayer requests here so you can pray through the week for each other.]

ASSIGNMENT:
1. Pray and ask God to reveal areas of your life that you struggle with in relation to worry. Create a list of these worries and then a list of how they can become concerns.

2. Pray through each area of worry, giving it to God and allowing the Holy Spirit to make some changes.

3. Pray for someone to hold you accountable to change.

Chapter 8:
Walk the Line: Anger versus Anger?

I'm Not Angry, Really, Really!

"You ALMOST killed me and my baby! Don't YOU know what you did? How DARE you, lady? You are crazy, CRAZY!!!! " Well, these were just a few brief statements from a lady who thought I had cut her off in traffic when in fact she had cut me off. I watched her stop her car, leaving the engine running, her child inside, car door wide open, just so she could walk over to my car and yell at me. She was screaming like a lunatic, barely making any sense. I kept asking her to calm down, "You have me mixed up with someone else, you actually cut me off in your anger. Ma'am, ma'am, do you really want your daughter to see your behavior right now? Do you really want the world to see your behavior? Ma'am, calm down."

As she drove off, I could feel that my blood pressure had risen, my heart was pounding, and my mind was swirling. I was so proud of myself! She had road rage and I had none. She lost it and I kept my cool. She made a fool of herself and risked the life of her child by leaving her car running and unattended. I was able to talk quietly and firmly without responding back in a defensive and angry manner. So, great, I have come a long way. But what also hit me was that I could have been her. I have been in her shoes. I have felt violated, harmed, attacked, accused, cut off, and stolen from, whether it was all in truth or what I thought was truth. And even though, in your deepest desires you hope to act like Christ and only get angry when it's the right time, your flesh is weak. I have made a fool out of myself many times. Yes, I am better than I was because of Christ, but each circumstance the Lord allows me to go through only tests me, grows me, and matures me.

So how do you know when it's okay to be angry? This woman felt that due to having her child in her car, she had a right to verbally attack someone she thought had almost harmed her. Is anger okay as long as you believe it arises out of truth? And what about people who frustrate you in general, such as your neighbor, workmate, or those you live with? Maybe they haven't done anything big like damage your car or cause you harm. Maybe they have a barking dog, they don't pick up their clothes, they're in a bad mood in the morning, or they talk too much in meetings. When is anger good... and when can it cause more problems? We must first start with the source.

Q: What makes you angry?

Q: Describe what has happened when you have lost your temper.

SOURCE OF ANGER:
I have found over the years that nine times out of ten, my anger (from sudden outbursts to being frustrated and irritated) stems from some underlying issue. There have been times I got mad at my family or friends, lost my temper, and of course, expected them to forgive. I can't tell you how many times I have lost my temper in traffic. And what about when you have lost something and can't find it and you need to leave for work. But if you take the time to really peel back the layers of how you are feeling, you will begin to see what the source of the anger truly is. Identifying the source will lead to a solution. You will be able to discern righteous anger from unrighteous, and then you will know the next step to take. You begin to realize your anger at your family is deeper due to things from your past. Friendship anger is because you have never held your friends accountable for their sin, so you allow it to frustrate you—causing you to sin. Traffic—it's life...you could just leave earlier...or losing something? Get better organized. Most of the time, our anger is not righteous or permitted; it's about "us" and our mess.

Q: So going back to the last question, when you shared about a time you got angry, take a few steps backwards and see if you can identify the source of the anger. Follow the sample below and write it out, sharing with the group.

For example: Traffic caused you to get angry, cutting off someone, and getting into a yelling match.
1. Peel the layers back.
2. There is always traffic where you live; so are you stressed due to leaving too late? If so, what caused you to be late? Did you stay up past your bedtime? Did you get distracted with TV, emails, social media, a phone call? Did something break at home? So, if you haven't figured it out at this point, go deeper.
3. If everything was the same last night and this morning but you are still angry in traffic, what could be the problem? Then you realize it was a phone call you got the day before that was bad news. It's the job you didn't get a week ago. It's dreams that have not been fulfilled.

It's God not answering your questions the way you want. Wow, so now you are starting to see the difference and can start to deal with your anger in a healthy way, getting help if needed.

UNRIGHTEOUS ANGER:
Unrighteous anger is anger that is self-focused—about winning your way whether or not the outcome is based on truth. Your goal is to control. Unrighteous anger reveals insecurities, selfishness, and fear in life around you. You can't fix it, so you yell at it, throw things at it, hit it, and ultimately destroy it.

Bottom-line: we hate that someone else has control of our situation. We hate that life didn't turn out the way we wanted it to, that we didn't get the job, the mate, or the promotion.

Unrighteous anger can also show up in unforgiveness of others as well as yourself. God is not saying that we have to forget what someone may have done to us (or even what we have done to ourselves), but holding onto that anger, that unforgiveness, will slowly kill you and others around you.

RIGHTEOUS ANGER:
I hear these words and think, "How can anger really be a good thing?" Thank you, Jesus, that some people are willing to stand up and say "no" to things that are immoral or unjust. They are willing to fight for the unborn, the neglected, and the ignored. When you are concerned over a situation, sometimes you reach the point where you know there needs to be action to make changes. This righteous anger keeps the situation, the problem, on the front lines. You don't give up in the fight towards truth.

Q: When have you had righteous anger?

Righteous anger can also be about your own situations when you are harmed, abused, or robbed. You have a right to be mad. It comes down more to how you react, how you verbally and emotionally respond. Sin is in this world. People are going to steal from us, the washing machine is going to break down after having it for one day, the line is still going to be long at Walmart, your food order is going to be wrong for the 3rd time, and yes, they should have done this or that, but didn't. The question to start asking yourself is, "How do you plan on dealing with it?"

Q: What are some steps you have done to help you control your anger?

The Fine Line Revealed:

Read Proverbs 26:4
Do not answer a fool according to his folly, or you yourself will be just like him.

Test Your Anger:
When you find yourself angry, aggravated, or frustrated, ask yourself where it's coming from. Take the time to count to ten, if need be, praying and thinking about how you are feeling. Vent in such a way that shares your frustration (to others or God as needed) in a healthy way. I cannot tell you how many emails I have written in anger and put in my draft folder, only to delete them later once I cooled off.

Read James 1:19
My dear brothers and sisters, take note of this: Everyone should be quick to listen, slow to speak and slow to become angry, because human anger does not produce the righteousness that God desires.

If It's Unrighteous, Go Deep and Find Out Why:
I get so overwhelmed by the many things I have to do. I feel like a rubber band pulled every which way. This feeling (based on truth sometimes and sometimes based on my

own failure to plan better, say "no," etc.) can quickly cause me to get angry with family, friends, and even total strangers. Unfortunately, I have burned some bridges with people due to anger that has been my own fault. I am thankful that over time as I find myself in those same places, I can recognize the source and quickly calm down. And when I find out the source, I choose how to fix or manage it. Remember to practice peeling the anger away so that you can figure out where the real source of the anger is coming from. Re-read James 1:19.

Note: Sometimes our anger is so deep, from so much hurt, there is not a quick solution. This is when it is critical to get some professional help. I love Christian counselors and think everyone should take the time to see one. Don't let the enemy continue to control your life. Do what you need to do to get better.

If It's Righteous, Have A Plan:

Read Exodus 34:6
And he passed in front of Moses, proclaiming, "The LORD, the LORD, the compassionate and gracious God, slow to anger, abounding in love and faithfulness."

When you are righteously angry, have a plan about how to handle things so God gets the glory. Make sure your anger is consistent with the holy and righteous character of God. I like to use Facebook to share my agreement with how abortion is wrong. I am known to like or share anything against those who support abortion. Also, as a teacher of God's Word, I do not have a problem speaking out against certain lifestyles, such as sex outside of marriage or any other sin that is in the Bible—not to condemn or destroy people but to draw them to Christ. To show them the freedom in following Christ and doing things His way. To show them His love.

Read Psalm 78:38
But he, being compassionate, forgave their iniquity, and did not destroy them; and often he restrained his anger, and did not arouse all his wrath.

Q: What is God asking you to do when you get angry at someone?

The Solution:

Read Ephesians 4:26-27, 31-32
"In your anger do not sin": Do not let the sun go down while you are still angry, and do not give the devil a foothold... Get rid of all bitterness, rage and anger, brawling and slander, along with every form of malice. Be kind and compassionate to one another, forgiving each other, just as in Christ, God forgave you.

Q: What does being angry do to us and others?

Read 1 Corinthians 13:4-8
Love is patient, love is kind. It does not envy, it does not boast, it is not proud. It does not dishonor others, it is not self-seeking, it is not easily angered, it keeps no record of wrongs.

Anger should not be sinful. Don't allow the enemy to take control by submitting to your flesh. Our goal as Christians is always to do the Father's will. As we spend time with the Lord, reading and studying His word, praying, serving, and tithing, you will begin to see how your anger will change from being all about you to being all about God. The focus changes from being about loving only yourself to loving others.

The mom who went supernova nuts on me was probably late getting to the store. She might have had a fight with her husband, gotten a bill she wasn't expecting, or found out her mom has cancer. The true anger wasn't what she thought I had done, but in fact, the pressure valve blew due to unresolved anger that she had. By not dealing with her anger, she allowed it to build up. I am just thankful that God had placed me in her life that day to remind her to calm down and realize what she was doing. Did she get my address so she could write me a "thank-you" note? Uhhh, no. But I did pray that she got somewhere and thought about what I had said, even going to God to ask for forgiveness and help with what was really wrong. Then she, as with all of us, will begin to heal.

WHAT ARE YOU GOING TO WALK AWAY WITH?
What is God saying to you right now?

[Close in prayer; option to list prayer requests here so you can pray through the week for each other.]

ASSIGNMENT:
1. Pray and ask God to reveal any areas of unrighteous anger and create a plan on how to deal with it so you can get healthy.

2. Pray for a friend/family member to hold you accountable regarding this anger.

3. Pray and ask God to reveal any areas of righteous anger and how this could be used to draw more people to Christ.

LEADER'S GUIDE

As the leader/facilitator, it is up to you to expand your discussion beyond the questions and scriptures that have been given to you. Take some time to pray and ask the Holy Spirit what additional questions, thoughts, and Scriptures you could use. You can also include video and movie clips, handouts, objects, and just about anything else you can think of to help teach the lessons. See below for some ideas/suggestions.

Before you start: Plan to start a week early to get to know your group. Conduct an icebreaker that is fun; provide snacks. Then do something that gets to know people a little better. Ask them to share more of their story/background. Ask them what they hope to learn from the study. Then assign them the first chapter to read and fill in the questions.

Ideas for each week:
• Create a resource list that included counselors, divorce and grief recovery services, drug addiction services, mentors, etc., whatever you think they might need as the study goes along.
• Conduct an icebreaker or warm up exercise for week. Icebreakers are simply to break the ice and warm up exercises are specific to the lesson. To purchase a list of over 125 proven ideas, go to www.FromHisHands.com Ministries.
• Divide the class into small groups of no more than four to get deeper into the discussion, allowing more transparency. Be creative on how you do this each week. You could divide by age/sex/background.
• Open in large-group prayer but close in small-group prayer (of no more than four). This allows folks to get to know each other, going deeper in their relationships, accountability, and community. You can decide as their teacher how to break into prayer groups—whether the same each week or different. Set a specific time to start and finish, encouraging groups that finish early to not talk, distracting others.

ABOUT KRIS SWIATOCHO

Kris Swiatocho is the president and director of The Singles Network and From His Hands Ministries. Kris has served in ministry in various capacities for the last 25 years. An accomplished trainer and mentor, Kris has a heart to reach and grow leaders so they will in turn reach and grow others. If you've ever heard her speak, you know Kris keeps the crowd captivated, shares great information, and motivates people to make a difference in the lives of those around them!

After graduating from North Carolina State University with a bachelor's degree in Environmental Design, Kris received graduate training from Southeastern Baptist Theological Seminary. She has been an affiliate staff member with CRU (Campus Crusade for Christ), taken leadership development courses, and coordinated numerous workshops and seminars.

Kris has written articles for or been featured in many magazines such as Lifeway's Christian Single and Home Life, Crosswalk.com, Single Matters, Charisma, plus radio and TV shows in the USA and the United Kingdom. She is also the author of several books, including her most recent, "Everyone Knows a Single Adult: The FAQs of Single Adult Ministry."

Currently Kris lives in Fuquay-Varina, North Carolina, but travels and speaks to audiences all over the USA and the world. She does not have a husband, children, or even a dog to keep her company, but she does care for a couple of healthy house plants. Her hobbies include making jewelry and karaoke singing (all she knows is "Crazy" by Patsy Cline).

To find out more information about how to bring Kris to your city, go to www.FromHisHands.com or www.TheSinglesNetwork.org, or call 919.434.3611.

From the Manger to the Cross:
The Women in Jesus' Life
by Kris Swiatocho
8 Biblical Models for Study

Jesus, Single Like Me!

With Study Questions

KRIS SWIATOCHO

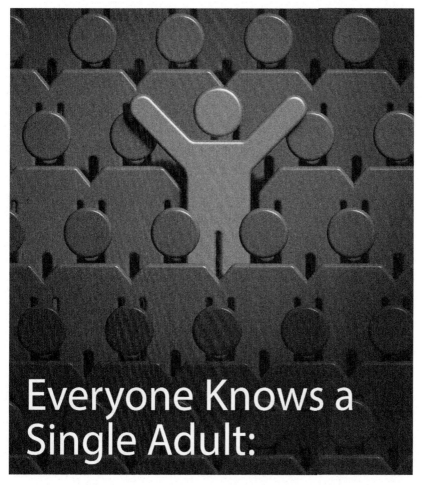

Everyone Knows a Single Adult:

The FAQs of Single Adult Ministry
50 Contributors | 100 Questions and Answers

Kris Swiatocho | Dennis Franck

Printed in Great Britain
by Amazon

84470919R20061